SERGEI RACHMANINOFF

FIVE PIECES (Op. 3)

Piano

ISBN 978-0-7935-5675-5

G. SCHIRMER, Inc.

DISTRIBUTED BY

HAL•LEONARD®
CORPORATION
7777 W. BLUEMOUND RD. P.O. BOX 13819 MILWAUKEE, WI 53213

NOTE

The FIVE PIECES for Piano, Op. 3 were composed in 1892, and dedicated to Anton Arensky, and published the following year by A. Gutheil. They became almost immediately repertoire pieces. Of the FIVE PIECES however, none became as popular as the PRELUDE IN C♯ MINOR, which is one of the most performed piano works ever written. It has had many extra-programmatic fables attached to its history, including the one that it is the composer's portrayal of Napoleon's invasion of Russia. Actually when Rachmaninoff was asked what inspired him to write the PRELUDE he immediately replied "40 rubles!" valued at about $20 at the time.

Although Rachmaninoff died and was buried in America (March 28, 1948, Kensico, New York) it was his ultimate wish to be buried in the cemetery of the Novodevichy Monastery in Moscow where friends and other illustrious artists of the 19th century and the recent past are buried, Gliere, Chekov, Ippolitov-Ivanov, Stanislavsky.

For this edition the first four pieces are edited by Luise Vosgerchian, Walter P. Naumburg Professor of Harvard University.

The final piece, SERENADE, has been edited by Alexander Siloti, Rachmaninoff's friend, cousin, teacher, and champion performer of his music. Siloti, himself a pupil of Rubenstein and Liszt, was remembered by Rachmaninoff when he dedicated his 10 PRELUDES, Op. 23 to him.

Five Pieces, Op. 3

I

Elégie

Sergei Rachmaninoff
Edited by Luise Vosgerchian

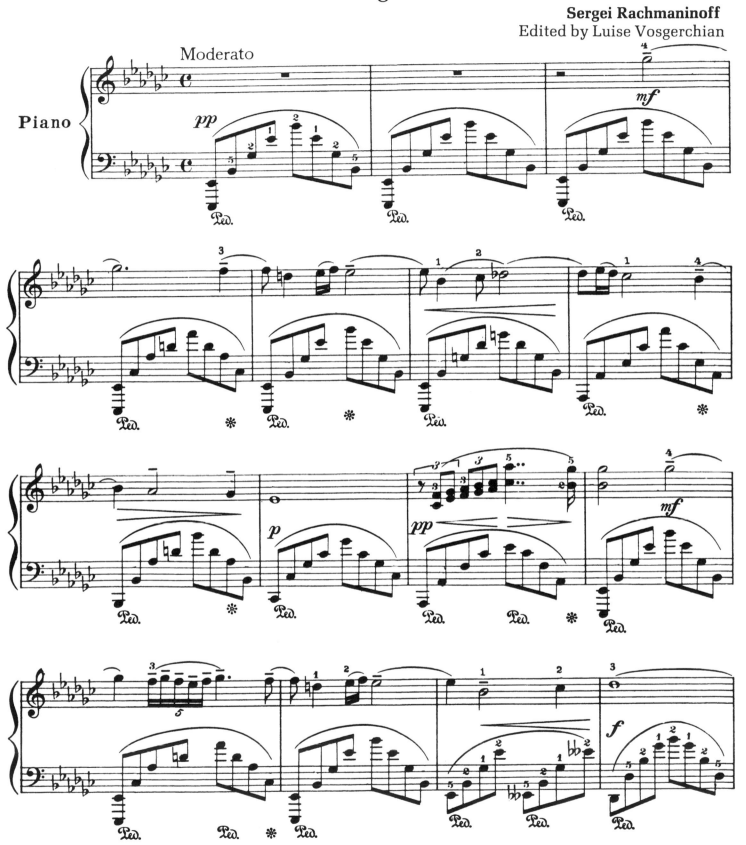

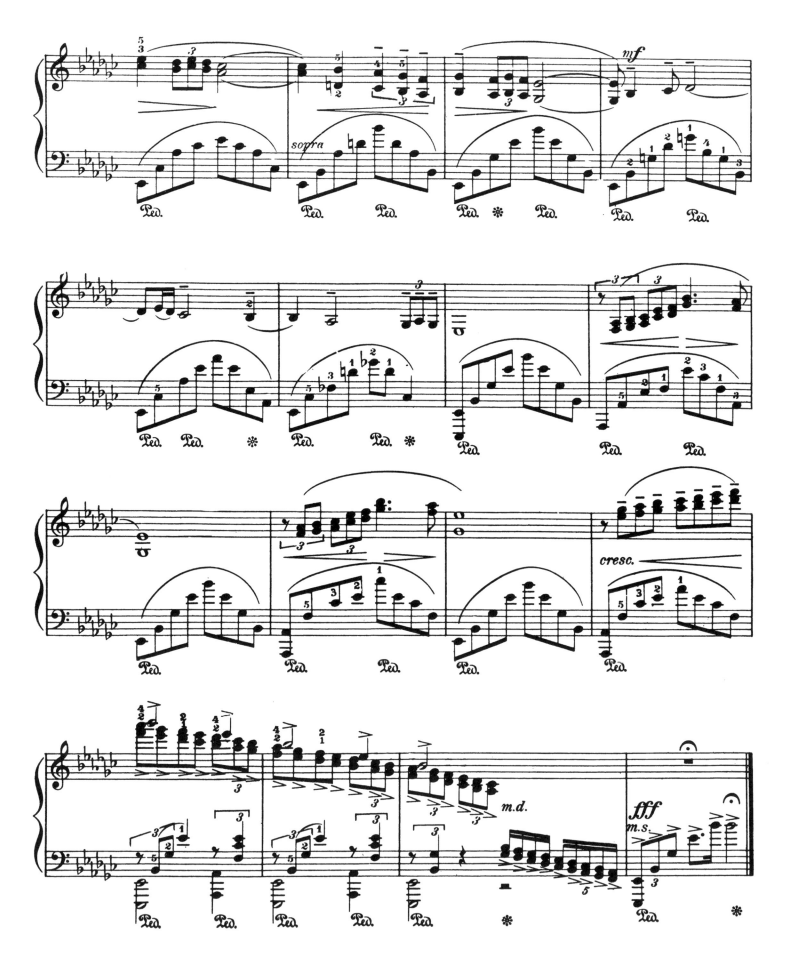

II
Prélude

Sergei Rachmaninoff

Edited by Luise Vosgerchian

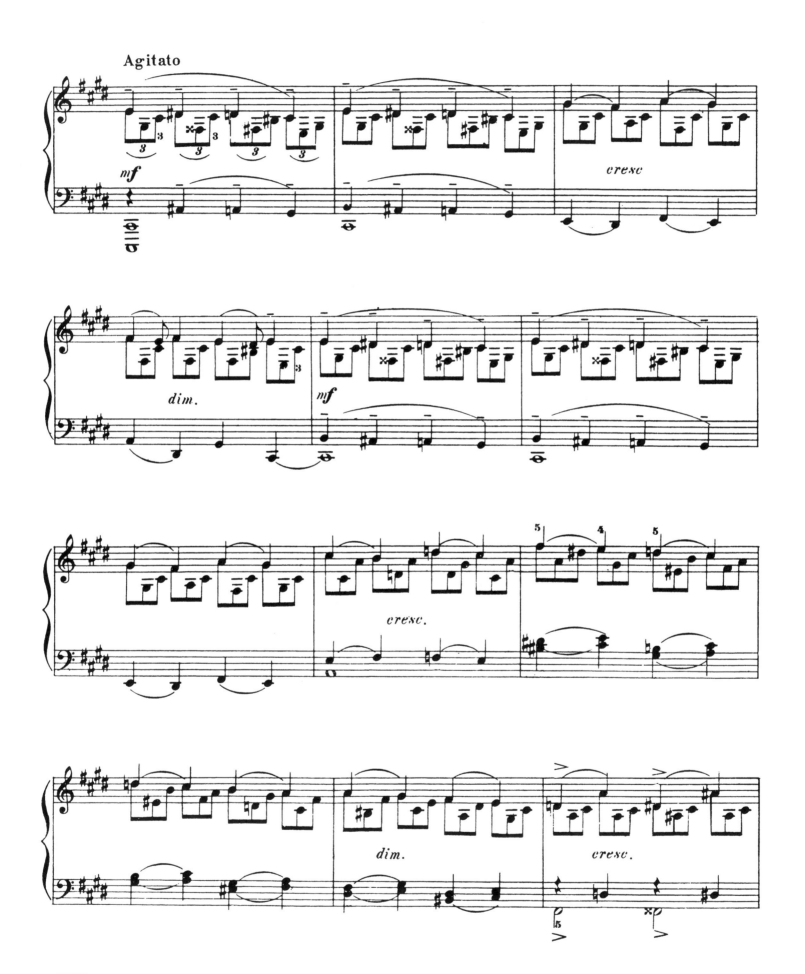

III
Mélodie

Sergei Rachmaninoff

Edited by Luise Vosgerchian

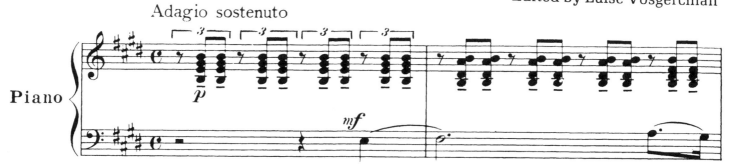

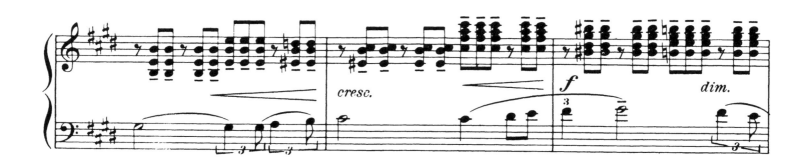

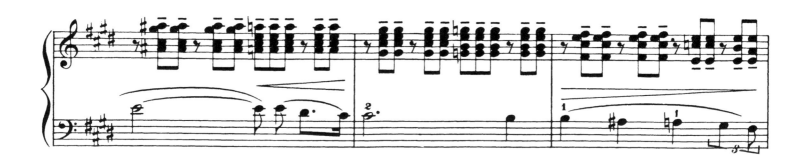

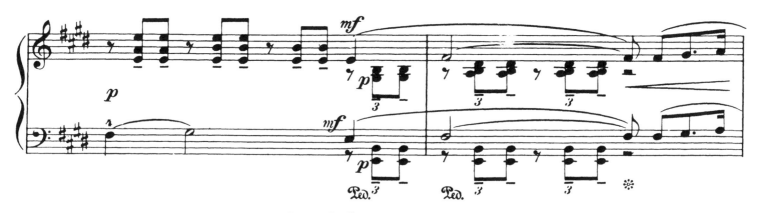

IV
Polichinelle

Sergei Rachmaninoff
Edited by Luise Vosgerchian

V
Sérénade

Sergei Rachmaninoff

Edited by Alexander Siloti

Tempo di Valse *(non troppo vivo)*

47602